# 30 Different Microphones in 30 Days

## #PauseReflectMoveForward

A book of poems about pausing, reflecting, and moving forward with your marriage or not from a bipolar perspective.

Holly DressON NOT Holly DressOFF

ISBN: 0692126406
ISBN-13: 978-0692126400

# DEDICATION

I dedicate this book to any woman who has paused and reflected and decided to move forward with their spouse or without, especially bipolar women considering divorce.

# CONTENTS

Preface     iii

Acknowledgments     xi

1   He Will Use His Power 4/18/18     14

2   A Blesson 4/19/18     19

3   I Am Number 1 4/20/18     22

4   Burst 4/21/18     24

5   Dreams 4/22/18     27

6   Permission 4/23/18     29

7   Believe 4/24/18     31

8   Undone 4/25/18     33

9   Unblock 4/26/18     35

10   Telling Myself 4/27/18     37

11   Gifts 4/28/18     40

12   Take Care Of You 4/29/18     42

13   I Am Less Stressed 4/30/18     45

14   Stabbed 5/01/18     47

15   About To Go Down 5/02/18     49

| | | |
|---|---|---|
| 16 | Clench 5/03/18 | 52 |
| 17 | Make Our Dreams Come True 5/04/18 | 54 |
| 18 | His Wife 5/05/18 | 56 |
| 19 | Alphabet 5/06/18 | 59 |
| 20 | Come Here Let Me Love You 5/07/18 | 61 |
| 21 | Russian Roulette 5/08/18 | 64 |
| 22 | There Will Never Be A Tonight 5/09/18 | 67 |
| 23 | I Wasn't Sure Which Way To Go 5/10/18 | 71 |
| 24 | Trust 5/11/18 | 74 |
| 25 | Left 5/12/18 | 77 |
| 26 | Win 5/13/18 | 79 |
| 27 | I Don't Belong 5/14/18 | 81 |
| 28 | React 5/15/18 | 83 |
| 29 | Tonight May Be The Last Time You Love Me 5/16/18 | 87 |
| 30 | Back 5/17/18 | 91 |

# PREFACE

I'm learning to have bipolar and all that that involves.
I was diagnosed January of 2017 when I was 41 while I was hospitalized after an attempted suicide and being baker acted.
At the time I wrote these poems I was 42 and self-medicating myself for bipolar.
During the 30 Different Microphones In 30 Days challenge I gave myself, I was contemplating moving forward from my marriage of 17 years, who just so happens to be my high school prom date and father to our four children.  We were at a point in our marriage or so I thought, where I needed to move forward and whatever that looked like.

As you'll see in this book of poems on my 30 day journey,  it is a roller coaster ride of emotions, which as I'm learning is a part of bipolar. I'm learning to recognize my extreme highs, extreme lows and what my triggers are.

Some of the poems may make you blush. Once you continue reading the 30 day journey not only will you be entertained, you'll have a closer look at my love of not only expressing myself through poetry, but how I love.

This book was designed to be read in chronological order so you can try to understand the fluctuating emotions in my bipolar mind.

My husband didn't show up on 4/14/18 for my 1st ever reading of my poems that I invited him to which just so happened to be at the place we had our reception after we eloped in Las Vegas on 2/14/01. I was hurt, ashamed, and aggravated all at the same time. Our marriage had been on and off since we started dating 26 years prior.

Thursday April 14th I read the poem titled **Redesigning**.

## Redesigning

When two people meet.
They lead you to your seat.
You order drinks.

You look over the menu.
Your thinking to yourself should you
continue?
It's been rough what you've been through.
You continue.
You order your meal.
And start thinking "This isn't such a big deal."
It's nice.
Someone paying attention to you.
Complimenting you.
You continue.
He's different.
You like that.
He's smiling.
All the while your pining.
Over once was.
How you'd gotten here.
How far you'd come.
You wonder if he could actually make you
cum.
It crosses your mind.
Because you've been doing it to yourself for
quite sometime.
You miss a few words here and there.
And wonder if he ever cared.
You get scared.
Thinking what you thought was love wasn't.
How could it have been?
Men!

You excuse yourself from the bar and say "I'll
be right back."
He says "I'm going to order another drink
would you like something?"
"A refill on my water in a wine glass" you say.
Boy this has been a long day.
You go to the ladies room.
Thinking they could really use a broom.
You wash your hands and check your face.
And wonder how you even got to this place?
Checking your face.
You knew you couldn't erase.
The past that's been holding you back,
And that's a fact!
You take a long look in the mirror and sigh,
And think of the man sitting at the bar if his
beard would feel good on your thigh.
Back to the bar you sit.
Again thinking "Is he the right fit?"
You continue talking.
He orders yet another drink,
And you start to think.
"I've been down this road before"
And you remember the chore.
And know you cannot and will not do that
anymore.
Dinner arrives.
You eat your salad.
And listen to the ballad.

He's new,
And the time blew,
Past you as he asked you,
"How have I lived without you?"
You blush,
Because you knew he had a crush.
You smile and your cheeks flush.
Oh what a rush!
It's been too long.
Something was bound to go wrong.
It did.
You noticed.
He seemed off focus.
You don't drink.
You knew it caused you to think.
Unclearly or not at all.
And wonder if a fairy tale was even real after
all.
He asks for the check.
And still you reflect,
On how you 1st met.
Was it serendipitous as you once had thought?
Or is it that you just got caught?
In the idea of,
Him being sent from up above?
You question.
And wonder.
And pray there won't be any thunder.
He walks you to the car and you insist on

driving.
His alcohol level was rising.
You protect yourself.
Better than you did.
For so long you had hid.
Those beer bottles piled by the sink in the
morning,
So he could count while you were pining.
Over him and what could have been.
If he only knew how much he meant to you,
Maybe then you would have made it through.
He closes the door.
Not able to explore.
All of you
For with him there will be no more.
Because now you know on a scale from one
to ten
You will never put yourself through that
again.

Out of being aggravated I felt I needed to do something to move forward. I came up with the idea of **30 Different Microphones In 30 Days** within the next couple of days.

I wasn't going to start the 30 day challenge until Thursday 4/19/18 as I was going to spend Wednesday evening the 18th with one of my daughters for her birthday. Her and I ended up spending the entire morning together on Wednesday 4/18/18. I took her for her drivers permit because she had turned 15 that day.

My husband and I had been separated and living apart for 9 months at this time. 2 of our children living with me and the other 2 with him.

She spent the evening with her dad and 3 siblings.

So I didn't mindfuck myself during that evening, I ended up finding an event which had a microphone and the journey began on the 18th verse the 19th of April.

Every day following the 18th I found an event with a microphone to use all over south Florida for 30 consecutive days.

I completed the challenge I gave myself and am sharing my thoughts and feelings from that 30 day roller coaster of emotions in poems which I wrote the morning of each of those 30 days and read the poem I wrote that day or evening whenever the event was scheduled.

Welcome to 30 days in my bipolar mind.

*Holly DressON NOT Holly DressOFF*

# ACKNOWLEDGMENTS

My mommy who is gone but never forgotten.
My daddy for teaching me how to move forward.
My husband for his love and patience.
My 4 children for their unconditional love and belief in me.

**Special thanks to**:

Sabrina Fajardo SabrinaFajardoTheBrandArtsan.com for the cover design

Carrie Childs & Elle Horigan of CarriElle's Closet for wardrobe

The Mistress of Ceremonies, Crystal Chanel, the owner of Press Release Marketing

Rebecca "Butterfly" Vaughns
TJ Hope
Ingrid B
Shirley Toliver
Jeanette Hickman
Comedian See No Evil

Jeanette Hickman "Hostess with the Mostest"

Terese Chunky Hill
Spittfiya Productions
Spoken artist

Mike Cintron
Wayne Felber

30 Different Microphones In 30 Days

## 4/18/18
## HE WILL USE HIS POWER

God damn he's a good fuck
But he brings me no luck
That night in his truck though
Damn he can fuck
I sat on his face and I tell you I am so grateful
that I could be in that place
But it didn't erase
The look on his face
When he's mad
And then you can see in his face he's glad
He made me feel that way
Why the fuck would anyone want to make
you feel that way?
At one point I thought I should be gay
But that's not the way that I play
I do wonder
Why there was thunder?
I honestly didn't know

I would end up sleeping with a man named -
uh-oh
He didn't show
Me the way to go
I have to find it on my own
Now that I'm grown
I don't have time to be pining
Or wining
Or crying
Or complaining
I need to be campaigning
I didn't know which way to go
And that my poems would flow
Now I know
This is my time to grow
I admit I kept getting under him
I knew there was no way to get over him
We went to the gym
Only thing I saw there when I went there with
him was him
I love that man but let me tell you what I can
And cannot do anymore
I'll tell you one thing I can't let him score
Even if he takes me by the shore
I love the beach
It helped me reach
And I'm telling you man that man he can
teach
You how to cum

And to come undone
It took me several different tries to know that
I was done
Several times I sat on that man's face
As much as I try to erase
Knew I could not replace
Question was why would I even consider?
He was put on this earth at this point of my
life to help me hinder
I thought of him often
Sometimes that included him being in a coffin
I didn't want that
But I'm telling you I couldn't help that
Now I can
I've proven it to myself that I can
You hear what I'm saying?
You will not be able to move forward if you
keep laying
Letting him tap that ass or sit on his face it is
never going to replace
The fact that he made you chase
Him over and over and over again
Why the hell would you want to put yourself
through that again?
What point are you trying to prove?
Because you couldn't remove?
I will tell you something right now honey
There are many men you can let taste your
honey

You know what you want you're a grown ass
woman
Take your hand and show that man that he
can
Pleasure you exactly the way that you need
him to
I'm telling you he will help you get through
Every once in a while you need to make a
man blue
Stand in your power
Do not ever let him see you cower
He will use it against you
When that court date comes
He will try to make you cum
And you'll let him
Because you're thinking you shouldn't have
left him
He'll get in your head and he'll get in your bed
the worst place of the two is that he's in your
head
You lose sleep
While trying to count sheep
What you should be doing is not continuing
He will keep on hindering
While you're considering
He will fill your head with lies
With all of the tries
And somehow turn it into your cries
You're worth more than that

That's a motherfucking fact
Don't let him see you react
He will use his power

## 4/19/18
## A BLESSON

Did you fall,
For his call
Right before your court date
He asked you for a date?
Were you part of his menu?
So he can continue to manipulate and
articulate
How did you not know it was too late?
You get caught and thought
That maybe just maybe it could work?
You had time to work on your twerk
You know that motherfucker is a jerk
You went over there without a mother
fucking care and because he wasn't giving you
any money
You took toilet paper from his place
because you didn't have any at your place
You took paper towels
You took leftovers from his house

You laid with him while he played with you
and the time flew
What in the fuck are you thinking?
I know he wasn't drinking, and neither
were you
Still you allowed him to lick and then make
you blue?
When he took you to lunch you were
hoping that he would munch
On you and yet you still continue.
Attachment?
It's stupidity plain and simple
Don't even think about his dimple
He will make you cripple
You have worked so hard to be where you
are at
Don't let him get none of that
You've become hard and you like that
That week? Was great it was almost too late
thank God you have friends who will tell you
what you need to hear not what it is that you
want to say
You do not have any longer to play
It is time for him to pay
Pay he will and even though he may give
you a chill
You know the drill
It has happened before and you remember
the chore

Please I beg you please close that
motherfucking door.
So one can open
I know you've been hopin', but woman you
deserve better
Someone to get you even wetter
That's all you need right now
Go out and get it
Because I'm telling you, you cannot let it
You will mind fuck yourself to death or
they're about
As long as you care about
Those eyes between your thighs
I'm telling you babe
You can find other ones
A really great guy
One who will treat you the way you feel
you need to be treated
Because for so long you have been mis-
treated
This lesson? I'm telling you it is a mother
fucking blesson
You keep confessing your love for him and
he will keep you stresson'

# 4/20/18
## I AM NUMBER ONE

I don't want to talk about my problems,
I want to solve them
Which means I can't let him
Get in my head
Or get in my bed
But I do want to place
This pussy right on your face
I don't want the drama
I got my own
Now that I'm grown.
And growing
Into what I'm not quite sure yet.
You can place that bet
That even though I do fret
I will never forget
Who was there for me when I needed them?
Or the one that left me crying in our bed
I realize now it has more to do with him than
it does with me.

I need you to let me be.
I need to know what it's like to be free.
So I can continue to be.
The best version of me.
Before we can ever be
Now scoot up on the bed a little bit more
I need you to explore
Just how my pussy contours
I know it's as sweet as honey
Please don't look at me funny
I'm out here trying to earn that money
For reasons you couldn't possibly understand
I've taken a stand
To fight wrong with right
In the middle of the night
For those that cannot fight
I will use all my might to get it right
But right now I'm trying to get me right
I don't want a relationship
Friends with benefits maybe
Don't treat me anyway other than a lady
I bet you anything that anybody that's had a
piece of me will never forget me
But first I had to forgive me
And all the wrong I'd done
And come undone
And learn first and foremost that I am
number one.

# 4/21/18
# BURST

I'm not gay
Maybe there was this one time
I can tell why men and women alike want
what I have
But you see this bald pussy is not up for
grabs
My name ain't Lucy
But you bet your sweet ass this pussy is
juicy
Why is it bald you ask?
Because it helps me feel pretty
And that helps me be witty
I gave myself pleasure through the pain
I was going insane
So I came
I'm quite good at it
In fact
4 times in 3 minutes?

Beat that!
I don't do it too often in the morning
Because of all the moaning
I don't want to wake anyone up
So I fill my mother fuckin' coffee cup
You see at this point of my life I'm grateful
I ain't got no time to be hateful
Now I'm going to school you
Pay attention
1st you lick the tip of your middle finger
And place that mother fucker right on your
clit
If you don't know where it's at
You better read up on that
Feel your lips as you move your hips
And if you have a dick to dip
Be sure to keep rubbing your clit
Bald is always better
This way when your pussy gets wetter
You'll feel better
Don't wait for him or her in order to explore
Give yourself more
Love you more
I know the chore that comes with waiting
Due to them hating
My pussy needs to be multiplicating
Are you sick of the lying?

To yourself more than him?
He always gave himself a trim
I know you liked to suck on his rim
But you cannot let him in
I know he feels good in your pussy
But when he leaves your bed he is stuck in
your head
You keep repeating the same cycle
Guess what?
You'll never have that motorcycle
You're different
He doesn't like that
But I tell you what
There are plenty of men who will like that
You have to love yourself 1st
In order to quench your thirst
I'm telling you
Make that pussy burst

## 4/22/18
## DREAMS

Can I rest my head on your chest?
I just need to rest
I know I am blessed
But damn sometimes I just get stressed
Let's not talk
Let's just lay here for a bit
Then maybe go for a walk?
My mind won't shut off
I need to get off
Let me sit on your face
I know you can erase some of my thoughts
Before I get caught
I know I have resting bitch face
Help me erase
Let me mind stop turning
Help keep me learning
About being the best me I can be
I am meant to be free

I like being alone
It shows me I've grown
What's next is unknown
But in the meantime
While I'm busting my rhymes
I'd like to keep a smile on my face
And remind myself never to chase
No not like in a horse race
But by keeping me out of the rat race
No I'm not like the others
I like to be under the covers
With someone to hold me late at night
And in the morning
And after my day
So together we can play
But right now I can't
And I won't
Because I need to be left alone
To remind myself how much I've grown
You see this is my season of preparation
For my next destination
Either be patient or don't
Because giving up on my dreams I won't

## 4/23/18
## PERMISSION

I kept talking about all the sex I wasn't getting
And guess what?
I received no sex
I kept saying how mean he was to me
And guess what?
I received anger
I kept lying in bed by myself begging him to
be there
And guess what?
I received loneliness
I kept saying how he wouldn't look at me
And guess what?
He didn't see me
I kept saying how much he drinks
And guess what?
He was always drinking
Now? I say I'm grateful
Ain't no time for me to be hateful
Now? I look for love

And now that's what I see
I say how much I love my life
And now I do
I'm telling you
In order to get through
You have to pull through
The mess
To be less stressed
And let another man take off your dress
And let him confess
His love for you
In order for you
To do you!
Figure it out!!
I'm telling you there is a way out!
I know it's hard to see
But you my beautiful friend are meant to be
free
Give yourself permission to change your
direction

## 4/24/18
## BELIEVE

As I went through this journey
I was learning
To hold my head up
And never give up
To do my best to smile
And not to cry
Somewhere along the way I met a really nice
guy
And decided to give him a try
Because I know he cares
And I know it scares
Because you know all those scares we have?
We have to repair
Take ourselves to the fair
And live to dare
To make our dreams come true
This I'm telling you
Will help us do

Whatever it is we want to
Because what's inside of us is dying to come
out
Get rid of those clouds of doubt
I know we've been torn inside out
But we only have one life you see
We have to make it count
Don't let your dreams follow you to your
coffin
Practice them often
Daily
Several times
I'm not suggesting us to commit any crimes
But while you're listening to my rhymes
Don't you remember the times?
Where you had the desires and the passion
To give and receive satisfaction?
Let yourself receive
So you can start to believe
It will help you not grieve
Of who you once were
I do concur
Who you once were?
Is still there
And I know that you care
Why don't you dare?
Because if you don't
Guess what?
You won't

## 4/25/18
## UNDONE

Do you have trouble relating in a relationship?
You know
How previous relationships you've been in
you were misunderstood?
You've tried several times to explain yourself
and not getting your point across?
Maybe a time of two you felt lost?
And it even cost
You your marriage?
Or two or maybe even three?
Maybe the problem isn't the other person?
Maybe it's you?
Please don't misunderstand me
A relationship has two people
One may be trying to communicate and the
other not receiving or vice versa
Is it due to previous relationships that you still
haven't healed from?

Past hurts?
Past regrets?
Do you feel a threat?
Or are you one?
It's important to come undone to figure out
how to put you back together again
To love yourself first
To be a good friend
A good mother
A good daughter
A good sister
A good wife
I know how much if feels like a knife
To be cut in two
Or three
Or four
And still wanting more
Try to adore
You
And all that you are
You've come so far
Don't reach back
Reach forward
And every once in awhile
Glance back to see how far you've come since
you'd been undone

## 4/26/18
## UNBLOCK

I associated pain with love
I was trying to understand if he was sent from
above
Like why now?
And learned that things don't happen until we
are ready
But now that this change has occurred how
do I know if it's the time
And why do I rhyme?
I know everything happens at the right time
I still mindfuck myself
And still want to hang trophies on my shelf
To prove to myself I could do it
I can get through it
I deserve to
I've been through
Some crazy shit
Not knowing if he's the right fit

Is giving me such shit
He's new
I knew
I need that
But how do I receive that?
My hat is off
I'm open
I'm letting the light in
But I'm
Blocking it
How do I unblock it?
The fears that I have
I worry about my dad
And if my kids are glad
I can make it through
And I can help you
Let's lock arms together
So we can fly
And accept a new guy
Give him a try
Because
You never know when we may die

## 4/27/18
## TELLING MYSELF

Don't get involved with anyone until your
divorce is final
Please I beg you
Feelings get confused
You feel like you're being used
Someone gets hurt
You don't want to be you
After all you've been through?
I know you will probably do it anyways
Hoping someone will end your dreary days
I promise you there are different ways
One day she lays
Next day she lays
The next day she pays
The price
Of doing her best to be nice
You may think twice
Or three or four or more

It turns into a fucking chore
You deserve more
You deserve to be able to trust
And separate the lust
Your mind will fucking bust
Everyone thinks you're crazy
And you no longer look like a lady
Your life does not need to be shady
Maybe just maybe
You can be your own baby
Take yourself out for a walk, go to the beach
go to the movies so you can reach your next
level
And be prepared for that fucking devil
He's trying to make you come on level
You cannot let him get to you
You have too much to push forward through
Don't pause don't reflect move forward
Do you hear me?
I'm shouting it out the roof top
You have to come out on top
You were not born for a mediocre life style
You have to file
For divorce
Follow this course
It will set you up for success
And I promise you someone will take off your
dress
You must first let go of the stress

Don't you want to impress?
Yourself?
If you look back on your life and you remain
his wife while you laid with him and thought
of him and thought of you
Only you can push through
Only you can move forward
Toward
Have you ever stopped yourself and ask
yourself what are you doing in the mirror?
What was your answer?
Did you even have one?
You need to add value to your life and let go
of being his wife
As I'm telling you this I'm telling myself

# 4/28/18
# GIFTS

Gifts
How many do you have?
Maybe you've forgotten?
You have several you know?
Not all may apply to you though
But you'll soon realize your gifts
And what doesn't fit
The gift of sight
The gift of touch
The gift of taste
The gift to feel
The gift of feelings
The gift of love
The gift of peace
Yet all too often we forget
I'm here to remind you
To find you!
You are worthy of all the gifts you have

And I wouldn't normally be here every day to
remind you
To simply just be you
Through your life I know you've surrounded
yourself with some people that have been
hateful
When you have felt that they should be
grateful
Them being hateful had nothing to do with
you
It has to do with them
And then
Once you realize this?
Your life can be bliss
Not without the work
And no I don't mean working on your twerk
It is necessary
But first
Love you!
Love all of you!
And whatever that looks like to you
That will help you get through
Do you
And whatever that looks like
Because you may just
Get it right

## 4/29/18
## TAKE CARE OF YOU

If he hears your cries
He wins
Pick up your chin
And let's begin
Your life
Now is your time
It isn't a crime to have a divorce
I know you wished differently about your
marriage of course
Now?
You suffer with remorse
Change your course
Please don't force!
Your love on him
Love on you
That will help you through
You cannot undo
The past

From your last
Go ahead and cast that real
Start to feel
Love
Look for it
Everywhere
I don't care
If you find it in wearing sexy underwear
But find it
Don't hide from it
Your worthy
And your hips are curvy
Your face
In the morning
Can never replace
The heartache
The earthquake that happened to your family
I know about Stanley
You don't have to hide
What you're feeling inside
But
Just this once
Give you a try
Love you
Make yourself happy
Instead of waiting for someone to do it for
you
Adore you
Love you

Find you
Hold you
And that pillow at night
When you're up late at night
It won't talk back
It will listen
To your condition
Won't tell anyone
Only you will hear those words uttered
Unclutter
Your space
Your mind
Your friends
Begin to mend
I do recommend Breathing
For receiving
No more grieving
It is time to start retrieving
Your hopes
Your dreams
Watch the stream
Of love
Of blessing
And let go of the stressing
Stop messing
With those who question you
And fail to mention you
Take care of you And whatever that looks
like.....

### 4/30/18
## I AM LESS STRESSED

I like to sleep naked
My night clothes seemed to smother me
I feel the need to be free
Free of the restraints
The chains that bound me
Thank God I found me
I was lost
In this big wide world
And it nearly cost me
My life
Remaining his wife
I couldn't hold onto him anymore
It seemed like a chore
And what a fucking bore
I cried
As he lied
On that couch
I had to figure me out
Now you want me?
After I'm gone?
You had me so long

But you did me wrong
And made me feel I didn't belong
I loved you
I still do damnit
But I couldn't handle it
Wondering
Waiting
Crying
Feeling like I was dying
So I left
Flew out of the coo coos nest
So I could rest
I know I'm blessed
And I enjoy having my body caressed
And being undressed
Right now I can't though
I need these rhymes to flow
To show me which way to go
You once said "you'll follow me anywhere"
The thing I realized is that you won't
So don't
Send me a song through text
Thinking you'll receive my best
Because now when I lay my head down at
night to rest
I must confess that
I am less stressed

### 5/01/18
### STABBED

I can't do you anymore
I can't do us anymore
There can be no more
This I know for sure
I was looking for a cure
To help me?
To let me?
Breathe....
In order to receive
And try to believe
Then learn to believe
In the possibility
To see
How could it be?
We were us for so long
And then it went wrong
I'm not sure when
Or where
I know you know I care

So don't you dare
Declare!
I didn't
I always did
I never kept that hid
I confessed
You digressed
And left me stressed
And lonely
And cold
And sad
Now?
I have dreams
And I believe
That we
Will never ever be
I cannot let it be
It hurts me too much
And this strength I have, I have to clutch
With everything I have
And never let my heart be stabbed
Again.....

## 5/02/18
## ABOUT TO GO DOWN

I swear his dick just fell into my pussy
I fight with that man
But he still can
Get to me
I was high
I know no excuse
But he got me loose
I let him lick me
Then I let him stick me
And then I took a shower
And then he brought me flowers
I let him in my bed
And I'm doing everything I can to not let him
in my head
I get choked up
On thinking of the past
And I get choked up thinking of......
The future?
There would be pleasure through the pain

But I'd have him
And he'd have me
And we'd be a family
We tried it once
Twice
Three times
Even four
It still seemed like there was more?
See the questions I have
They brought me to this place
Where I cannot erase
The good
The bad
And how he licked on my hood
Was so good
I'd been so misunderstood
It doesn't mean he'll be by my side to the end
It just means for today
I'm not a mind reader
I can't predict the future
What I do see in the future,
Is a creature
That I've been making all along
So I created a song
"Shaking out my couch on the carpet"
To remind me of how I've lived
When he didn't give a damn or so it seemed
So now?
I'm working on my plan

Does he fit?
Or do we quit?
I'll tell you one thing
Not while he's sucking on this clit!
My life is an adventure
I want to revel in this roller coaster
Maybe I'll used this bolster
To hold me up
While he's licking me up
And down and all around
Because this time around
He needs to go down
No time to clown
This #PauseReflectMoveForward shit is
about to go down

# 5/03/18
## CLENCH

When I'm not talking to you I'm talking to
him
How could it have been?
I don't like to be alone
Somehow I've learned to sleep alone
And not mind it
To help me find it
His lips on my lips
As I move my hips
And then he places his hands upon my chest
Somehow I seem to rest
As he clenches
Onto my soul
I won't let him keep me from my goal
But I will let him in
I like him there
For so long it seemed he didn't care
I like to dare

With this love affair
Or is it attachment?
Entrapment?
Or real?
He knows how he makes me feel
I know it's a big deal
But if this is what I need to do to heal
Let me deal
And you be there
Or don't
Because giving up on my dreams I won't

## 5/04/18
## MAKE OUR DREAMS COME TRUE

I'm going to bring that mother fucker to his
knees
And this pussy?
Is what he will please
I told him to get on his knees
And I asked him nicely if he would lick me
please
He obliged while I was high
He's an asshole kind of a guy
But has always been the apple of my eye
Others try
And I try to deny
These feelings I have inside
But I can't
The lust I have for him
No one can dim
He still shines through
And gets to me
Lord please have him continue to respect me

Have him say things to me that is music to my
ears
Erase my fears
And
Never make me tear
This is my year
Better than last
Will our love last?
Yes
Will we be together while it does?
Cause
That I don't know
I'm going with the flow
I'll tell you one thing he won't ever let me go
This I know fo' sho'
Is it healthy?
Will him staying make me wealthy?
The answer is no
I will
Am U classy? Yes
But you know we have all been a little trashy
We are all jus out here trying to make a little
cashy
And make our dreams come true
This #PauseReflectMoveForward message is
brought to you
By the one and only
Holly DressON not Holly DressOFF

# 5/05/18
## HIS WIFE

Not enough people meditate they medicate
How is it that I'm supposed to articulate being
on that shit?
It made me not sleep
Gave me the sweats
I lost my smile
And I went to file
For divorce
Of course
My marriage got off course
I didn't want to force
My feelings on him
So he went to the gym
I worked on a plan
To show the world I can
No wait not the world
Just me
I needed to prove it to me

That I can learn to be free
Of the burden
And to no longer be a burden
To myself
And create my own wealth
Place my trophies on that shelf
To remind myself of all the things I can do
And what I brought myself through
My accomplishments
And astonishments
Shocked everyone
They wanted to know how it is that I didn't
come undone
And figure out how I had won
It came down to one
Damn I am having so much fun
I know I need to get back to my run
And he has felt like he needed to pick up a
gun
And make sure it's done
But he hasn't
And he won't
Because killing someone he knows he won't
He's a big wussy
And while he's eating this pussy
He calms down
And learns to receive
All of me
And together he believes we can be free

I'm not quite sure how that would be?
What I don't understand is why he didn't
come to me?
Confront me?
Listen to me?
Instead of listening to others
He always wondered who I was with under
the covers
He didn't have any brothers
I was with others
And I knew I couldn't give myself completely
Because that man has me completely
And as we move swiftly through life
I still remain his wife

# 5/06/18
## ALPHABET

We tried the alphabet for the 1st time
While he was in between my thighs
And to my surprise
H-o-l-l-y multiplies
My orgasms
And he has me spasm
My whole body shook
As he took
Me to another level
On the bed there was a bevel
And out came my little devil
Let me revel in our glory
As I do my best to figure out this story
It's a mystery
You see
I know we are meant to be
But will it last?
As I compare and contrast
Please don't move to fast
I need this shit to last

I see the forecast
In the past
I saw
Cloudy days
And years of rain
Storms
That seemed endless
And left me breathless
Now?
I see rainbows and
Pots of gold
As this story unfolds
And my body explodes
As he holds
Onto me
From the front
I listen to his grunt
As he drills this cunt
And I smoke on my blunt
Don't front
Don't hate
Let's love
And believe in our love
That it is sent from up above

## 5/07/18
## COME HERE LET ME LOVE YOU

"Come here let me love you", he says
As he grabs my ankles and pulled me to the
side of the bed.
He buries his head between my thighs
And I look down at his eyes
He tastes me
And I feel him
Start to lick around my rim
Up and down
And side to side
His tongue
Moves
And my body moves
My head is thrashing
While his face is smashing
Onto my flower pillow
Lord tell me we won't willow
He holds my thighs

And forgives my lies
He always seems to surprise
Me while he's there
How is this fair?
And please don't you dare
Pretend you don't care
This is not truth or dare
How can you not tell I still care?
I'd much rather you articulate
Than me masturbate
I spent so much time alone
I still have so much left to do I feel as if I
need a clone
You're helping me through it
I know you knew it
Am I helping you?
For us to continue?
I do admit I like to be on your menu
But is it the right thing to do because of what
we've put each other through?
Who knew?
This could be
As you hold me gently
And then grab me rough
Please tell me our love is enough?
You're tough
Well so am I
I don't necessarily want to be with another
guy

However, if you start to treat me badly
I will gladly
Move forward to the next
And then you will be called my ex.

# 5/08/18
## RUSSIAN ROULETTE

I'm trusting you with my heart
You're worried that my legs will part
We knew from the start
We were both going to be torn apart
We may have married too soon
I didn't know about the moon
And how it would affect me
Or how I'd let you get to me
Same for you.
We cannot undo
What's been done?
We used to have so much fun
The memories we made
The trips we took
And now this book?
Who knew we would both become obsessed
And stressed
And scared

And lonely
Damn I love you
I know you love me
Are we really meant to be?
Or is it we cannot see?
Past those eyes?
Past the widows peak?
When I look between my thighs and your
there
I know you still fucking care
There are some things that need a tweak
I'm tired of being weak
I am now strong
I know I belong
I don't like using tongs to get the things I
cannot reach
It's been you for so long
Maybe just maybe this will turn into a song?
A movie?
Of all the things we've done to each other
To show the world we still want each other
Need each other
Like no other
We've been down this road many times
There always seems to be a U-turn
To go back to where we've been
We have both sinned
I've forgiven me
I still think you need to forgive you

Before you can ever forgive me
Me forgiving you?
I'm doing my best
And I know my best can be better
So we can beat this weather
And promise to never
Ever
Let each other go
And kiss under the mistletoe
I've had my Christmas tree up all year for a
reason
Because I believe in miracles
This has certainly been a season
Give me one reason I should stay
And continue to play
This game of Russian roulette

## 5/09/18
## THERE WILL NEVER BE A TONIGHT

I liked it better when you said you didn't like
me
That way I believed.
And knew I wouldn't be deceived.
Now that you say you do?
How can I believe you?
After all you put me through?
Why am I even questioning?
Is this the day of reckoning?
I know now, I matter
My thoughts
My feelings
Me reasoning
My seasoning
My intelligence
My elegance
My orgasms

My smile
My hair
Are all here to stay
This contrast is trying to weaken me
Your words?
Are making me question you
Why now?
Like what the flying fuck?
That night in your truck?
I'll never forget.
The kids we made and continue to grow?
They will know this fo' show
Their mother is not to be played with
Or laid with
Unless you can prove it to me that your
worthy of me
Without putting your tongue between my legs
while I sit on my throne
Which just so happens to be on your face
You doing that does not erase
This place?
Where I'm at?
I can breathe
You get me all choked up
But those times that we fuck?
You were in luck
Because I needed to get off,
My broom!
I sure hoped you wouldn't finish too soon

Damn you can make me swoon
Make sure you tune
In
To see me
My stories not done
I did come undone
Now watch me rise
As I close my thighs
For good?
Yeah right
Not tonight, or tomorrow or the next day
If I want to finish my 30 days you'll have to
wait
Because this book
Will not be fucking late
Now you want a piece of me?
Or is it a piece of my new found freedom?
You can't possibly want to build a kingdom
Again?
The one we had crumbled
And left me humbled
And alone
But now that I've grown?
I've learned FINALLY!
I don't need a man
I need me
You?
You've had your chance at this romance
Is this your last chance?

It is
So hold onto your jizz
Because there will be a quiz
This is the game of life
You're playing with your wife
You better act right
Or there will never be a tonight

## 5/10/18
# I WASN'T SURE WHICH WAY TO GO

I wasn't sure which way to go
I felt as if I was turned inside out
I'd talked to so many people about what I was
experiencing
Not realizing it was hindering me
I tried reading the positivity
And tried to let things not get to me
It wasn't working
Still I kept working
To try to figure it out
I had so much doubt
How could I live without?
I needed to get out
To grow somewhere else because I was dying
No amount of water could have saved me
It would have drowned me
I needed to be replanted
I forced myself to do it
To help me through it

And those that were too
I found I wasn't all alone
I didn't want to talk about my sad story
I wanted to talk about what could be, what
would be and what will be
I forgot about me because of he
I loved him more than I loved me
I couldn't see
Me
Now?
I want to climb a tree
Be free
Of attachment
Due to the enchantment
Not sure how it ended up that way?
Lust?
And I gave him trust
With my heart
To never part
I believe I did my part
But I'm the end I had to depart
I couldn't do it anymore
I ended up on the floor
Now this mountain that I'm climbing
I will continue to climb
While I rhyme
And in time
I will heal
Knowing how much a big deal

It was for me to be real
Now that I know what that feels like
I hope one day to be right
For now
I'll continue to learn how
To not only help me
But to help others
Which makes me better
Through any type of weather......

## 5/11/18
## TRUST

After all was said and done
He re-proposed to me
Got down on one knee
I said yes
But cannot digress
Where he slept that night
The week was great
We stayed up late
That date?
Was perfect
But I don't know for sure how to let go
How to move forward?
What does that look like?
I think I need some wind therapy
Maybe the air will get in between my ears
And erase all my fears
And stop the tears
We were together for years
More than half my life

I was his wife
Last night?
I felt that something just wasn't right
I felt it inside my gut
And then it registered in my brain
Please don't tell me I'm going insane
Because this way I cannot remain
Maybe I'll go shopping for another domain?
Because I have to move forward
To show others it can be done
You have to do more than just run hun
It takes
Practice
And patience
And sleepless nights
Several fights
Screaming
And yelling
And sobbing
And breaking
Why oh why does my world keep shaking?
Is it to wake me up?
To knock some sense into me?
Into us?
I don't trust him
I don't trust us
Me? I have to trust
Because I am the only one who can make my
dreams happen

I can't wait for him, or her
I have to keep practicing
Forget about relaxing
I can't
I don't want to
What I want to is move forward
I promise I'm doing my best
But my best doesn't seem good enough
I need to prove it to myself just how tough
I am
To continue on my plan
That man?
God please don't present me another man
who will distract me from my dreams
My goal was to stay married
With kids I would carry
Till death do us part
That ring he gave me?
I threw it out the window
I know we will never rebuild that trust....

## 5/12/18
## LEFT

I was the oldest woman who was on stage last
night and the night before and the night
before that
I had the shortest hair
I arrived on my own
I love being on that microphone
I had the pleasure of meeting several new
people
It felt like home
Being there all alone
I've learned to like me
'Bout time if you ask me
I believe there are entirely too many people
Living in this world who aren't doing the
things they want to do
Because of worrying about what others think
Be careful not to blink
Because one day you may be on the brink

Of losing it
Or having it all
I choose to stand tall
Even though I sometimes fall
I want to recall
The pleasure I created through my pain
I was going insane
Years of tears
Now I want to hear years of cheers
For me
For who I am
For who I was meant to be
Not remain who I once was
Cause
I am not who I will be
I really can't wait to see
Who I will be
Laughter is best
It helps you be less stressed
Tears are important
To figure out which is better
You must experience both
This roller coaster ride is no joke
You must smile on what you once had
To get to your glad
Otherwise
You'll mindfuck yourself to death
And look around and have nothing left

## 5/13/18
## WIN

I felt like I deserved it
Looking back was it really worth it?
I suppose so
So I can get to know me so
I can teach them
How not to do life
To live
And give
And be free
Is what's meant to be
But you see
Without pain we wouldn't know pleasure
My love for him I could not measure
He doesn't treasure me
Not like I would like it to be
We have this pattern
Him and I

The more and more we try
I learn to get by
We have to say goodbye for good
Or do we?
I don't know what is truly meant to be
But you see
I lust that man
I love him
But I don't like how quick he snaps on me
Constantly
So quick to let me go
Right when we show
The kids we can
Figure out a plan
Then the world shakes
It tries to give me updates
That I don't deserve to be snapped at
I don't deserve to be cursed at
I don't deserve to have holes punched in the
wall right beside my face
How did I get to this place?
I know if I was to erase something
Even one little thing
Especially the ring
Everything would be different
But it isn't
And I can't
And I won't
Let him win

## 5/14/18
## I DON'T BELONG

If heartache didn't exist
Neither would love
Or so I think
I'm used to love hurting
How do I stop my heart from hurting?
Maybe I overthink?
It's quite possible
To achieve
The impossible
That man!
I don't know how he can
But he can
Make me wet and fret
At the same time
How much higher on this mountain do I have
to climb?
To survive?
And thrive?

This heartache of mine
Somehow
Someway
It feels so divine
I rhyme
To make things right
Sometimes I'm wrong
And feel like I don't belong

## 5/15/18
## REACT

I'm not sure how you're going to react
So I didn't tell you the whole truth
Can we sit in a photo booth?
Capture some more memories
Maybe dream about Bentley's?
You're not too friendly
Can we mend me?
How about you?
I did what I felt I had to do
In order to make it through
You've been my boo
For as long as I can remember
Remember that September?
When you walked in
And I looked up
I knew right then there was no giving up
At the time your truck was small
Not sure how you fit being so tall?
You've always had a way to make things fit

And seem legit
Then one day I called it quits
I used my wits at the time
Man I was blowing my fucking mind!
I didn't write then
I just kept asking myself when?
When will he change?
When will he see things my way?
Not knowing that wasn't the way
I should've sat with you
Come to you
In order to help us get through
But I didn't
And neither did you
What was I to do?
I cried
Too much
I talked to everyone
Accept you
You didn't seem to want to hear me
Didn't you know how dear you were to me?
How could you not?
But see
I've learned to see me
Completely
I still don't understand some of the things
that I do
That's helped me get through
I never meant to hurt you

I swear I didn't know what to do
So I left
And I still cried
Then I looked around and there was no one
to dry my eye
So I
Ran
I meditated
I created
A peaceful place
Without a trace
I tried to erase
But I couldn't
We shouldn't
Even be together right now
Maybe if we do
We can show the world how
That true love does exist
Even though you've used your fist
While I've made a list
Of all the times I got dissed
I didn't think of you
And what you might be going through
Damn you're tough
But you know what?
I'm tougher
I do like it a little rougher
While we are on top of the cover
We are great lovers

Can we try to be friends?
We've had responsibilities from the get go
Neither one of us know how to let go
So do we?
Or don't we?
Either way
I'm enjoying the ride
And I'm going with the tide
Let's hold hands and glide
Through the rest of our lives
With me as your wife.

## 5/16/18
# TONIGHT MAY BE THE LAST TIME
# YOU LOVE ME

Tonight may be the last time he loves me
Can this really be?
How come I didn't see?
How come he didn't see?
Why didn't we see?
He connected us
To have them
To grow them
To grow each other
And I ended up under the cover
With another
It's ok
I've forgiven myself
God forgave me
But will you?

We will have to see...
You see I'm working on forgiving you too
Because deep down within
We love each other
We laugh
We yell
We scream
We end up being mean
We both have dreams
But at different times
And now with these rhymes
We won't have to suffer at times
I know where Pause Reflect Move Forward is
going
It's not just knowing
It's believing
In order to start receiving
The trust?
Is an issue
For both of us
We both like to cuss
And we've made a fuss
We've explained our story a thousand times
Maybe a thousand and one
To our friends and family and we end up
being the ones shun.
It is because as much as they try to
understand
They can't

And they say they do
But they don't
No one knows how to walk in our shoes
Know the path He wanted us to walk
And talk
But we do
We keep moving forward
Or at least we try to
At times we were stuck in pause
And then spent entirely too long reflecting
What we haven't done is moved forward
I'm asking you tonight
If you would do me this favor?
"Will you love me like you're going to lose
me?
Or will you bring up the past and not let our
love last?"
There are some parts of our story
That are anything but glory
But we have this chance
At a new romance
Me and you
Together we can make it through
Let's just say "F.E.A." (Which means Fuck
'em All)
While our love withstands all
Let them call
Us names
And say we're insane

And I'll remember the day you came
To my rescue
I don't know how I'd live my life without you
Tonight may be the last time you love me

# 5/17/18
## BACK

I'll do the laundry tomorrow
I want to live for today
I'm tired of the heartache and sorrow
That came from yesterday
I'm not concerned if you pay
I have always found a way
My ways need to change
And have the courage to rearrange
My sad days
Lift myself up
When there's no one around to pick me up
Find ways to heal
While I deal
With this mess
Maybe that's why I've always loved cleaning?
I like making things right
In the middle of the night

You not being there
Showed me you didn't care
How dare you leave me there!
Those nights I was all alone
All I could do was stare
At that empty space
My mind couldn't erase
The fact I always felt like I had to chase
Maybe that wasn't the case
That's what it felt like to me
And you didn't seem to want to try anything
differently
What was I to do?
To try to get through
I was lonely
You were supposed to be my one and only
But I got lonely
I needed to be held
Touched
Rubbed
Caressed
And fucked
I didn't seem to have any luck
They say bad luck is better than no luck at all
I didn't know I was going to fall
More and more in love with you
I love that you're so tall
Can we erase it all?
Start over?

Will you promise to bend me over?
And lick me from front to back?
And tell me you're coming back?

# ABOUT THE AUTHOR

Holly DressON
mission is to help people move forward from what is
holding them back without other people's opinions and
judgements getting in the way. She believes Pause Reflect
Move Forward can be applied to all aspects of your life.
And feels it is essential to apply
#PauseReflectMoveForward to the life you've always
dreamed of.

Follow either hashtag #30DifferentMicrophonesIn30Days
and #PauseReflectMoveForward on social media.
Also for her blogs and merchandise visit
www.PauseReflectMoveForward.com